MW01093731

# Praise for *Living Happily Ever After—Separately*

"Happily ever after doesn't always have to mean living under the same roof! This enlightening and useful book offers an alternative approach to marriage in the 21st century for those who love their spouse but can't stand living with them!"

~ Arielle Ford, author of *The Soulmate Secret*

"This beautifully written book is the soulful journey of a couple who, rather than settling for a dysfunctional marriage or divorce, have trail-blazed a third way—living separately and keeping the family unit together—a creative possibility for couples wrestling with two unacceptable choices."

~ Mary Elizabeth Marlow, author of
*JUMPING MOUSE: A Story About Inner Trust*

"In sharing her personal journey, Ms. Stoessel presents a creative approach to salvaging love and commitment, the essence of marriage, when living together is eroding this as well as one's sense of self.... I'll be giving it to clients struggling in their marriages and considering divorce when there's still some love, trust and respect, but too much sacrifice of self involved in living together."

~ Catherine Johnston, Ph.D. psychologist

"'Irreconcilable differences' are the cause of thousands of divorces in this country, as the common separation agreement will attest to. This book demonstrates that irreconcilable differences can lead to an outcome other than divorce.... [Stoessel's] story gives us hope, enlightens our imagination, and strengthens our resolve to create something new for ourselves when our relationship is faltering, rather than letting it end. For anyone thinking divorce is the only way out—read Stoessel's story, and think again."

~ K. Catherine Albano, family law attorney, mediator

"This book speaks for a generation that was determined to do things better than their parents, to be true to themselves in achieving personal goals *and* creating loving families—to have it all.... Lise Stryker Stoessel gives us a glimpse into the pain and joys of her generation's struggle in the family with gender roles, financial realities, and the lack of models for positive alternatives to the patriarchal model.... The hope we find here is that it isn't too late; the 'boomers' are still working on changing old and destructive patterns that have kept past generations from both freedom as individuals and the connection we long for with others. Getting past the either/or thinking that has told us we must resign ourselves to what is, or reject it totally, opens up new possibilities for creative and fulfilling relationships, families, and communities."

~ Susan Oberman, family and community mediator

*Living Happily Ever After—Separately* is a rich account of honoring the profound call to connection that doesn't fit neatly into our culturally prescribed boxes. Ms. Stoessel's commitment to her soul call as a guiding purpose for these connections and her unique way of honoring both her own voice and her enduring love for connection with her family is a powerful testimony that can offer creative alternatives for individuals looking for hope and professionals walking with people facing relationship distress."

~ Annmarie Early, Ph.D. Licensed Marriage and
Family Therapist

"Poignant and insightful work.... It's about hope, and learning through living, and trying again.... I applaud her and her family's bravery and would gladly recommend this read to individuals and couples on the brink who are not quite ready to throw in the towel (or who at least wonder if there are any options of last resort). There are certainly some pearls of wisdom and beacons of hope in here for them."

~ Tziporah Rosenberg, Ph.D. Licensed Marriage and
Family Therapist

# Living Happily Ever After
## Separately

by

Lise Stryker Stoessel

 Brandylane

ISBN 978-0-9838264-1-5

Library of Congress Control Number: 2011940585

Cover illustration by Lisi Stoessel

❀ *Brandylane*
Brandylane Publishers, Inc.
www.brandylanepublishers.com

I lovingly dedicate this book to my three daughters,
Lisi, Julie, and Susanah,
who have made it All worthwhile.
May their journeys into family life be even more
rewarding than mine has been.

# Table of Contents

# Acknowledgements

The genesis of every book is a journey, and the path that led to this publication encountered many helpful souls. I would like to thank the therapists who assisted Emil and me in so many ways over the years: Carol Ann Bush, Scott Sparrow, Margery Daniel, and Cathie Platt. My psychologist-friend Cathy Johnston read the first draft and gave it a thumbs-up. Two of my editor-buddies, Lucy Ivey and Anita Holmes, helped me spruce up the manuscript before I submitted it to publishers. Tamurlaine Melby, my editor at Brandylane Publishers, has been a dream: her suggestions have been spot on and imbued with wisdom and creativity. Sarah Vogelsong also helped with editing; her keen eye helped bring the manuscript to completion. And I am grateful to Robert Pruett, the publisher, for recognizing the potential of my work.

I would also like to acknowledge Cris Arbo and Joseph Anthony (my ex-wife-in-law and her husband). They have joined Emil and me in putting the welfare of our daughters foremost and have been loving and supportive friends to us in untold ways.

Deep appreciation is likewise due to my mother and father, Betty and William Stryker (English majors both), who instilled in me a love of language, as well as the desire to communicate effectively.

Most of all I would like to thank my husband, Emil, for many things: his deep devotion to our family, his willingness to truly listen when things got rough, his unswerving dedication to spiritual ideals, and his openness to new possibilities.

# A Marriage Proposal

Once upon a time, an idealistic, hopelessly romantic young woman met the dashing man of her dreams. He swept her off her feet in a whirlwind courtship and they were soon engaged. The happy couple exchanged their vows in a candlelit chapel surrounded by family and friends. Their storybook wedding held all the promise of a lifetime of love and devotion.

And then they woke up.

The life that they awoke to was not the stuff of fairytales (although there was a stepmother involved...). It had turned into a difficult journey of opposing needs, competing desires, and toxic bitterness. But wait! This story doesn't end there. After years of matrimonial discord, they did, in fact, find a way to live happily ever after ... by living separately.

You hold in your hands the story of how my marriage took me from a fairytale courtship to the depths of despair, and how I found a way to rescue myself and my family by reimagining and redefining my marriage. After twenty-three years of struggle, my husband and I agreed that we could no longer live together. But underneath all the pain and disappointment, we realized that we still loved each other and wanted to find a way to renew our relationship.

And so began our journey toward a healthier, happier life for ourselves and our family. Here you will find my own account of this journey, as well as chapters written by my husband and our three daughters. More than a memoir, this book ponders the institution of marriage, our social expectations of it, and its altered function in today's complex world. Last but not least, this is a self-help guide designed to assist you in finding ways to apply what I've learned to your own situation.

Since writing this book, I've encountered so many people who are at a crisis point in their marriage. I see their pain, their desperation, and I know how it feels—I was there. Nearly all of them have proceeded toward divorce because they didn't know what else to do. I want to help change that.

Whether you've been married for years, are just starting out, or are aiming to avoid the rocky path other relationships have taken, this book is for you. I offer it in the hope that among these pages you will find the inspiration to look at your union and your future with new eyes. Perhaps in reading our story, you will find the means to heal your relationship and get your life and happiness back on track. After all, you too deserve to live happily ever after!

# PART 1

# My Story:
# The Fairytale and the Anti-Fairytale

CHAPTER 1

A Separate Peace

I dial his cell phone.
 "Hello?"
 "Hey there. Where are you working?"
 "In Farmington."
 "I'm making minestrone. What time do you finish?"
 "I can be there in about an hour."
 "'K, see you soon."
 I'm standing at the stove, steam rising from the soup pot as it dances a little elemental dance in the light from the cooker hood, the smell of herbs and garlic wafting over me as I stir the vegetables, simmer the broth. Renaissance music is playing on the stereo; the strains of viola da gamba, recorder, and violin accompany me from the living room as I work in the otherwise quiet house. Felix the Betta, my fishy companion, swishes and wriggles in his watery world, peeking and darting from between the fronds of his plant forest in the fishbowl above the sink.
 Baskets of every shape and size adorn the window valance; pots hang from the wrought-iron wall rack; the cupboards are full; the counters are clear. The kitchen is peaceful, clean, well

stocked and well ordered, ready to come to life under my creative direction.

As the soup simmers gently, developing its heady bouquet, I take a big white china plate and arrange a salad for us: romaine lettuce, frisée, artichoke hearts, sun-dried tomatoes, pumpkin seeds, pistachio nuts, dried cranberries, salt, pepper, extra-virgin olive oil, balsamic vinegar. I carry it to the dining room, turning on a soft light on my way, and place it on the tablecloth. My napkin here, his there—across the table where he likes to sit, regarding me.

I hear the key in the door; he comes in, stomps his dirty work shoes on the mat, sloughs off his jacket, leaving it on the hall dresser. He gives me a little hug and kiss, walks past the kitchen, washes his hands.

"Smells good. I'm hungry."

We sit down to eat and talk about the day.

I had a good day at school. My nursery classroom was loud and bustling, full of life, activity, invention, joy, and struggle, the stuff that grows sturdy children. The most important lesson we're learning at school is how to catch our coughs and sneezes in our elbows, because while sharing is a wonderful thing, there are some things that are better kept to ourselves.

His day was good too: tearing out his customers' kitchen, finding surprises underneath the rotten wood, reworking the plans accordingly, being treated to a fresh fruit smoothie, sharing in the praise of their children's schoolwork.

Dinner is done, and we take the dishes to the kitchen. He lays the fire while I wash up.

We sit on the loveseat, watching the flames flicker and crackle. I sit beside him, my legs across his, my head leaned into his sturdy shoulder. His arm enfolds me. We watch the fire and muse, talking now and then.

"Have you heard from Sanah?"

"Julie called yesterday."

"Lisi and Jack will be coming for the holidays."

He looks at his watch and sighs.

"I have to go soon."

"Noooo," I whine. "Not finished cuddling. Wait until the fire's done."

"Okay, five more minutes."

We walk to the door together. He puts his jacket on. A kiss and a hug goodbye. I follow him out to the van. He turns to open the door, but I pull him into a final hug. He gets into the van, turns the key. I go back inside and watch from the door. He pulls around the cul-de-sac and I blink the porch light, in signal, as he drives away, up the street.

In our twenty-seventh year of marriage, we have finally discovered our key to wedded bliss: living separately.

# CHAPTER 2

# Wed.Lock.

1984. After about six hours of marriage, I began to realize that Emil and I were not made for each other.

At the age of thirty, I had a college degree, had enjoyed a volume-full of adventures at home and abroad, had "interviewed" many, many men, and had a heart full of dreams and aspirations. Life was good, the horizon was wide, and I intended to build a happy and healthy life for myself and my family-to-come.

Emil had moved to town to be near his two little girls. His wife had left him for another man and had brought Julie and Lisi, then two and four years old, with her. As it turned out, I cared for two little boys (working as a nanny), a coincidental complement to Emil's family.

Emil and I met at church. I had spotted him right off. He was well built with sandy brown hair and green eyes with just a little bit of sparkle. He was handsome in a relaxed and comfy sort of way, and he had good hands. I can tell a lot about a person by studying his hands. Emil's were strong but soft. The allure was deepened by his slight German accent. In fact, I had long held a fantasy that the man of my dreams would be a European carpenter. During a brief chat we discovered that we were both potters. As it turns out, Emil had even hauled a kick-wheel down from New Jersey in his recent move. He invited me over to see his pots, and we soon planned a couple of outings together. Sometimes his daughters would come with us. I knew that I wanted children someday, and as I watched them together, his tenderness and devotion to his girls went straight to my heart.

It didn't take long for us to realize that something was afoot between us. We didn't resist the sweep of emotion that led us into a very deep, intense romance. Every evening after I put the boys to bed, I listened for his lilting whistle coming up the drive. He brought his guitar and serenaded me in my alcove room. We shared all of our thoughts about life, all of our dreams for the future. He brought me organic peanut butter and mayonnaise; he wanted me to be strong, healthy. He wanted to take care of me.

Then we decided to marry. We had both seen enough of life and love to know that our union was singular, a gift. Months later we stood at the altar, our family and friends gathered to witness, Lisi and Julie in their long, fancy dresses, mounting the altar steps, bearing our wedding rings.

There was no money for a honeymoon; Emil was earning seven dollars an hour doing carpentry with some friends. We had rented a little bungalow one block from the ocean, and I worked quickly before the wedding to make it into a welcoming home for our family. There was a bedroom for Emil and me, a bedroom for Lisi and Julie, a living room, a bathroom, and a sliver of a kitchen. The friends who had lived there before us had left us a lot of their furniture, including their waterbed. As it turned out, the waves on that bed had followed their marriage to a rocky shore; they were in the process of divorcing, their three boys dividing time between mom and dad. Emil and I would re-christen that bed; we'd chart a course for fair winds and calm seas.

On our wedding night the bedroom was festooned with candles, and I ringed the bed with our wedding gifts as a circle of blessing around us. This was my *wedding night*, the moment I'd anticipated since I was a little girl, with all the dreams and expectations that had been waiting for fulfillment, and I had set the stage for storybook romance.

We got ready for bed in the darkened room, and I went to light the candles.

Then Emil spoke from the bed.

"Do we need all those candles? I don't want to be breathing that smoke all night."

So much for romance.

In the weeks before the wedding, I would awaken from awful dreams, each one a variation on the same theme. I would dream that I was engaged to a man whom I didn't know, didn't like, didn't want. But I was bound to him and didn't know how to extricate myself. I was miserable. I felt helpless, trapped, friendless, alone.

In the morning I would wake up and, after a moment, realize that no, it was Emil to whom I was betrothed, and I would feel awash in relief and joy. Emil was my prince. He was handsome, he was learned, he was a dashing European, he was romantic, he was a devoted father, and we shared the same hopes and ideals. I had waited for my prince, and he had come at last.

Yet there I stood, in our bedroom, on our wedding night, with the match in my hand.

"Do we need all those candles? I don't want to be breathing

that smoke all night."

It was a small thing, a conflict of preferences, but fairytales allow little room for disappointment. At that moment came my first awareness of the fantasy in which I had enclosed myself.

My prince was, perhaps, not all I had imagined.

Do all little girls cast their dreams for the future in the language of fairytales?

Many of the women I know did.

Walt Disney was our guide on the path of destiny: The gowns, the tiaras—every hair sleek and shiny in its place—with waltzes playing in the background. We would be lithe and lovely. We would be adored, beloved, caressed. Our princes would come and deliver us from the shadows of loneliness, of disregard, of anonymity. Our days of longing, of sadness, of struggle, would end. Our princes would carry us to their castles and we would live in peace, joy, and harmony forever.

All this would be ours if we waited for the Right Man to come.

But then came the '60s and '70s, when we marched for equal rights and hailed Gloria Steinem, Betty Friedan, and the legions of women's liberators as our leaders. Then we dutifully set aside the fairytale fantasies of hero on horseback and damsel in distress.

Or did we?

Or did that fantasy just go underground?

*I submit that while in our conscious lives we rose to the call of human evolution that demanded equality for all in every way, deep within our souls, in the silence of our interiors, the archetypal fantasies endured, quiet but compelling.*

Two imperatives at work. Two imperatives that would battle

each other and confound our lives. We want the fairytale—to be loved, cherished, and nurtured—*and* we want the freedom to be individuals, with a world before us in which to grow and express ourselves.

Ever the practical man, Emil, with his disdain of indoor air pollution, dispelled my fairytale illusion on our wedding night.

And then I woke up.

# CHAPTER 3

# Making the Best of It

And when I woke up I found that I was newly pregnant. I found that I was a wife with a household to run. I found that I was a stepmother to two needy little girls, one of whom was mad as hell, convinced (wrongly) that I was the reason that her parents were apart.

In short, I found that I was no longer myself, the driver of my life, but an operative in the lives of others. Not only had I given up the fairytale, but in addition, without realizing it, I had surrendered my life, turned it over, to the needs of this family.

Which might have been endurable. Except that Emil woke up too.

When he woke up, he found that the woman he had married was not fitting neatly into the space vacated by his former wife. This new wife was confusing. She wanted more of his attention than he could manage. She worked hard to win over his children and got downcast when they were scornful. She was emotional. Was it the pregnancy? Or would she always be so sensitive and exhausted? What on earth did she want from him? Why wouldn't she be reasonable?

Emil's way of dealing with these challenges was to withdraw emotionally, which, in turn, made me desperate.

I was pregnant for the first time in my life. I was now locked into the life I had chosen so blithely, and suddenly I found that I was married to a stranger. Who was this man in my bed, my house, my life?

I recalled those dreams...

I was cast into a sea of despair. When Emil went off to work, I spent my days weeping, pulling my hair, and finally, in desperation, I implored God to help me. I was so deeply ashamed. I could not confide in anyone. I had been so proud of our love, so convinced of its rightness, its destiny. And now it was ruined—in ashes.

After some months, with the progress of my pregnancy, I began to emerge from the darkness of despondency and found my footing. My belly grew round and full. The moment of quickening, when I first felt my baby move in my womb, brought an entirely new sensation, a keen awareness of new life within me and, along with it, a sense of determination. I would grow this little being. I would nurture this baby with all my love and intention. I would turn away from the ruin of my marriage toward a vision of motherhood.

Emil and I went to a birthing class, and, learning those techniques, going through those exercises together, we began to build a new bridge between us. The bond of marriage had been wrecked, but the bond of parenthood was being forged. And with the advent of our first summer together, we sweated through our daughter's birth, at home in our bedroom, in that bungalow by the sea.

And he was again my prince. He cleaved to my side throughout the pains and travails of my labor. For a moment he stepped away and I cried out for him. I needed him so deeply, with every cell of my being. He rushed back and said, "I'm here." And when our daughter emerged, we held her and he wept.

1985.

It was a new day. Having started this journey as embittered partners, we rejoined each other as devoted parents.

# CHAPTER 4

# Differences and Discontent

As the years went by and the girls grew up, Emil and I journeyed over a long, rugged path together. There were good times, to be sure. Sometimes they lasted for months. The good times were founded on the traits we had in common: we are both serious spiritual seekers; we both love to travel and experience new cultures and languages; we both place great importance on health in a holistic way; and we both treasure our children.

But inevitably one of us would say or do the wrong thing and the relationship would descend southward at a precipitous pace. Because I was a very sensitive and easily wounded person, a small provocation would burst through the trap door to the deep, dark well of my discontent. It was very bleak down there.

In those moments, our differences and disharmonies would engulf us: He tends to be a hermit; I am outgoing. He is a worrier; I am optimistic. He is a Spartan; I am a decorator. He is self-contained; I need and offer affection. He guards his territory; I invite people in. He likes his routine; I crave new experiences. He is practical; I am aesthetic. He grew up in a quaint farm village in Germany; I grew up in the bustin'-out sixties in urban America.

His cup is half empty; my cup is half full.

We have some essential qualities in common, but in many ways—ways that count—we are opposites.

So when one of us was tired or depressed, the shadows gathered and the battles arose. We would quickly lapse into old bad habits. We would get so wrapped up in our own needs, our own unhappiness, that it became a competition. Who felt more challenged? Who felt more abused? Who felt more exhausted? Who had sacrificed the most? And once the friction began, it took on a life of its own, driving us into a rut that was almost impossible to get out of.

I began to deeply resent him. With both of us stewing in our own despondency, there was no possibility of being kind to each other or being supportive. Instead, there was blame.

I blamed him for robbing me of my life—for tricking me into marrying him, for he surely did not turn out to be the prince who came whistling to my window those summer evenings. I blamed him for wanting to dominate me, control me. I blamed him for not caring about what I wanted, for erasing the joy from my life. I felt used and exploited, and worse, I felt invisible, disregarded.

He had his own list of resentments. He blamed me for withdrawing my affection. He blamed me for not being supportive of his work-life. He blamed me for not regarding him with the respect and appreciation he deserved. He blamed me for not providing a happy, welcoming home for him to return to after a hard day at work. He blamed me for not being the loving, devoted wife that he thought he had married.

We both became isolated, lonely, and needy in our marriage. The marriage was not feeding either of us; rather, it was eroding and exhausting us. It had entrapped us both.

# CHAPTER 5

# What Brought Us Together?

In my more philosophical moods, I would ponder the more transcendent picture of our union. If there is a reason for everything that happens to us (and we both believe that there is), why on earth did we come together at all?

I didn't have to think this one out for very long before I came up with the answer: the children. I believe that I was drawn to Emil in order to raise his, and our, children. I believe that it was a destiny that I had agreed to before taking on this mortal coil. I have come to believe that, in fact, my destiny with the girls was a much stronger magnet than my destiny with Emil.

It was February 1984—a few months before I met Emil.

I arrived at a Valentine's Day party. There was a table by the door with a long list of people on a sheet of pretty paper. Next to the list there were little note cards and colored pencils. The directions said: *Write your name on the list, then choose another name and write that person an anonymous valentine.*

I looked down the list. There were many dear friends on it.

But midway down was a name that stood out, almost calling me: Cris.

Cris had moved to town a couple of months before with her two little girls. The previous autumn she had fallen in love with Francis and left Emil. Likewise, Francis had left his wife and children. Cris and Francis were "visionary artists," and together they felt sure that it was their destiny to be joined.

I met Cris at church shortly after her move. She had not received an altogether warm welcome in our close community, and yet something told me to reach out to her. So I picked up the pencil and wrote her a note. I don't remember exactly what I said, but it was something to the effect of, "I know this transition must be hard for you, and I want you to know that I'm sending kind thoughts your way." I didn't sign it, nor did I show her any special attention that evening. But somehow she knew it had been me, and it meant a lot to her, especially since Valentine's Day is also her birthday.

In the weeks that followed, I decided to reach out to Cris and her daughters. They and Francis were staying in friends' spare rooms, moving around every few weeks. I brought them groceries a couple of times and visited with the girls. Lisi was a mischievous little sprite at four years old, with Shirley Temple dimples and a mop of golden-red hair. Julie was a little blond pixie, two-and-a-half years old, who followed her big sister around like a shadow, doing and saying everything according to Lisi's direction. Lisi coined the moniker "Lisestryker" (one word with a choppy cadence) for me, and Julie would repeat it with glee.

Two months later, Emil moved to town to be near his girls. We met, fell in love, and in the months that followed, planned a future together. Lisi and Julie were the ring-bearers at our wedding; Cris sang a song for us during the ceremony.

Later that evening, I spotted Lisi hiding under the piano with her thumb in her mouth. Something big had rocked her world.

Julie was a passionate, fiery child who desperately needed me to love her and to demonstrate at every turn that I loved her as much as I would come to love my own child, Susanah. Lisi, on the other hand, kept me at arm's length. She already had a mother with whom she was well bonded, and I was extraneous. She was always respectful and kind, but she never truly let me in.

Susanah, born the year after our wedding, was my soul's beloved. I adored her from her first breath. From a young age, Susanah's family and her home have always been paramount to her. We are a lot alike in our demeanor and our relationship to life. Our time together is effortless, tender, joyful.

I realized that it was my soul's destiny to raise these children—to love them, advocate for them, enjoy them, struggle with them. In my youth, after college, I'd had dreams of going to graduate school and becoming a psychotherapist, but I'd set them aside to do this work that was before me.

Now the children are grown. My job is largely done. I stuck it out through those long, unhappy years to provide a coherent home for them, to keep the family together, to offer them strength and stability.

I wish with all my heart that it could have been a happier home; I truly do. I wanted nothing more than to give my children the benefit of a loving family, something that I never had as a child. I did my utmost. They got the best I could give. They got my love and devotion. I willingly gifted them the best years of my life.

And now...what to do? With the children grown, does one eject the unhappy marriage? There were many times when I considered that option, but something always told me to be smarter than that. Somehow I knew that there was more work to be done—on myself and on the marriage. I had to try to find a way to make it work.

CHAPTER 6

My Life, My Space;
His Life, His Space

I t's 2010.
It has been three years since I moved into my own place, about
ten minutes from our family home, on the other side of town. I live
in a modest townhouse with vaulted ceilings, a bay window, and
a wood-burning fireplace. My living room has French doors that
open out to the deck. A regal spruce tree, where the birds make
their nests, stands sentinel at one corner of the deck. And beyond
the spruce lie the woods, with a little stream that gurgles along,
glistening in the afternoon sun.

Upstairs there is my bedroom, Susanah's room (where the girls
stay when they're in town), and my studio, stacked from floor to
ceiling with bins full of all the accoutrements of my craft work.

I have a big basement too: a spacious guestroom with sliding
doors that open to the patio, the perennial shade garden, and the
woods beyond. There's a laundry and storage area, and Emil, with
Susanah's assist, built me a bathroom down there, so that I could teach
a little home playgroup for my nursery students during the summer.

My home is quiet and peaceful, lovely and welcoming. People come in and exhale, relax, unwind. Amid the carefully chosen adornments, there are also empty walls. The colors are muted, soft. A large, carved wooden angel blowing the herald trumpet sits atop the white mantle, flanked by hand-carved wooden pine trees on either side. The easy chair and loveseat are upholstered in lush, dark, botanical fabrics that enfold you in a dream of the primeval forest.

Across town is our family home—Emil's house now. There are two work vans and a Toyota sedan in the driveway. Beside the driveway there is a pile of discarded plumbing parts waiting to be recycled. You walk in the front door and are greeted by boxes of things that either need to go to a job or have just come from one. In the middle of the sitting area there is a big, brown box heater pumping warm air into the cold room. On the end table and one chair there are stacks of half-read books. Behind them is the big oak bookshelf with books stacked in all directions, a scattering of picture frames, a few candles, a trumpet mute, some random screws and bolts, a guitar pick.

In the kitchen there are a few dishes in the sink, a crusty skillet on the stove. On the counter there are empty plastic bags, breadcrumbs on the cutting board. Bottles of vitamins and supplements stand in rank and file across the back.

This is Emil's home, his domain now. The girls are grown and fledged. And now that I am no longer living there, he can have his things exactly where he likes them. He works hard for a living, providing well for his family. He loves his work, and in return he enjoys the devotion and appreciation of his customers.

After years of struggle and territorial warfare, I came to the realization that he deserves to have a home that suits him—a place of peace, comfort, and renewal.

And so do I.

## CHAPTER 7

❧

# What Do You Deserve?

I t's 2007.

I'm in a session with my therapist, Cathie. I began working with her the previous summer after I blew out one of the discs in my lower back. My doctor gave me a book, *Mind Over Back Pain,* which postulates that all chronic back pain is the result of stress—stored anger, anxiety, frustration.

I've had yet another blow-up with Emil. They happen so often that it's hard to keep them apart anymore. They're often about money, that outer token of our insecurities. One such argument, which happened several years before, provides a good illustration.

Lisi had come over, telling us of her hopes to go back to school and complete her college degree. She wondered whether our offer of $5,000 per year toward college expenses still held in spite of the three-year hiatus she'd taken.

Emil stammered for a minute, and I chimed in, "Of course it does. Your education is important, and we want to support your efforts."

Emil balked, grumbling, "I'm not made of money, you know."

I retorted, "I know, but this is what we agreed to offer the girls, and Lisi is entitled to it."

His response: "Well, it's easy for you to say, you never lift a finger to help me!"

(As you may imagine, that was the wrong thing to say.)

"Never lift a finger?! I raised your f***ing children!"

(This was also the wrong thing to say, particularly in front of one of said children.)

I stormed off, furiously brushed my teeth, got ready for bed, and slept in Susanah's room. With the hair-trigger pulled, thus began yet another battle in the ongoing cold war.

Cathie gets me to talk about my feelings:

*I feel so trapped. I can't take this any longer. I can't bear the thought of living with him another day. Our house is a toxic stew of bickering and bitterness. There is no more tenderness between us.*

*He is distant, aloof, totally absorbed in his work and his books. He never asks how I am, what my day was like. He never suggests we do something together, go have some fun. And when I do go out with friends, he's sarcastic and angry if I wake him up upon arriving home.*

*As for me, I will confess my share too. I am cold and sarcastic with him, withholding intimacy. I don't bother telling him about what I've been doing because I know he'll say something that will annoy me. I regard him with disdain and haughtiness. Happiness is a bird that flew this coop a long time ago.*

"What is keeping you from leaving?" Cathie asks.

I answer, "Two things: the money and the family. Besides the fact that I can't afford to support myself, I can't bear the thought of rending this family. I can't bear the thought of losing the girls." Tears pour down my cheeks and my breath comes in sobs.

Cathie listens, thinking.

"But ... what are you modeling for your girls?"

What am I modeling for my girls?

*What am I modeling for my girls?*

I am showing them that marriage is a nightmare. I'm showing them how to be miserable. How to be bitter and resentful. How to give up what sustains and nourishes them. How to be fearful. How to surrender their life to someone else's dominion. How to lose their sense of entitlement to happiness.

I realize that I have stumbled upon another, more subtle biological clock: the one that says, "You're fifty-two, the children are grown, *isn't it time to have the life you deserve?* If not now, when?"

Cathie's question was the turning point. It was the key that unlocked the door to a healthier future for all of us.

# CHAPTER 8

❧

# What Had Become of Me?

2006. The year before…

Susanah, my niece Gabi, and I were visiting my dad and his girlfriend in Arizona. We took a side trip to Sedona, where I looked up an old flame, James. James and I had had a yearlong relationship full of passion, dreaming, and goofy fun. We hadn't seen each other in some twelve or fourteen years, and this was a sweet reunion. James took us up to the Red Rocks for a hike.

We were walking along, and James remarked to Susanah, "You know, your mom always knew how to have fun."

It stopped me in my tracks.

He was remembering the time that we roller-skated through the grocery store at one o'clock in the morning. Or the time that I threw him a surprise birthday party at his jobsite. Or the time that I invited him out dancing after we'd first been introduced. Or the April Fool's joke when I'd surreptitiously switched places with the guy in the sleeping bag next to him and moved over for a cuddle.

*I had been fun. I really had.*

*What had become of that person? Who had I turned into? Would Susanah wonder who he was talking about?*

What had been a lighthearted reminiscence for James became a touchstone for me. I pondered those questions and all of the implications for many days to come. What had happened to my life?

Then and there I realized that I wanted my life and my identity back. It had been too long, and I wondered whether I was coming dangerously close to the point of no return. Would I be able to revive that youthful, energized, fun-loving life explorer? I wanted to like my life again. I wanted to like myself again. And even more importantly, I wanted my children to discover *who I really was.*

CHAPTER 9

❧

# Is This Family Disposable?

S o. You might be wondering, *If your marriage was so miserable, why not just divorce like everyone else does?*
Well. There are those two reasons that I cited to Cathie:

### ❖ *Money*

Emil and I have worked hard to raise our children, send them to the right school (a Waldorf school), feed them the highest quality foods. He is a self-employed builder; I am a Waldorf teacher. We have a very modest income. We have always lived frugally, buying used clothing and furniture, economizing wherever possible. We have put a little money aside for retirement, but neither of us has a retirement plan per se. I could not imagine finding the money to pay the lawyers, let alone working out a "settlement." I tried to imagine getting another job, but then I remembered my back injury and the stress factor, and I realized that I would be trading one misery for another. The trade-off would not be a good one.

### ❖ *The family*

Our children have always been the top priority for both Emil and me. Not only do I esteem each one as an individual, I have also devoted so much of my being to raising them that I am very identified with them. Lisi and Julie lived with us full time from the time they were in the second and fourth grades, visiting with their mother for school vacations. I was their primary parent all those years, for better and for worse. We played, fought, suffered, and frolicked together. And Susanah, Emil's and my daughter, has been the light of my life from the moment of her birth. When I tried to imagine what might become of those bonds with divorce, it felt like a very deep violation.

Then there is a third, more important reason to avoid divorce:

### ❖ *We love each other*

It's no longer an I-need-you-and-you-need-me sort of love. The need thing had quickly devolved into a competition of whose needs were more compelling than the other's. Now it's the love of two mature people who honor the good and the noble in one another. It's the love that first illuminated our recognition of kindred souls in each other. It's the love that enabled us to regard and admire each other's tremendous strengths and virtues, even in the midst of our cold war. It's the love that brought us together and planted the seed for the family that we have grown, with all of its brambles and weeds.

And in recognizing that love, we realized that it is a gift, and that it is not disposable or easily substituted.

There are other reasons too:

### ❖ *I can't bear the notion of my extended family being a thing of the past*

I am so identified with my children, my home, my in-laws, even Cris, Emil's ex-wife, together with her current husband, Joseph, and her other daughters, Arianna and Alina. I don't want to imagine severing those ties. Back when I did contemplate divorce, I used to imagine how it would feel to be walking downtown, seeing friends in familiar places and being "a divorced woman" with a different identity, rent from those who used to be an intrinsic part of my life. It was abhorrent. Just imagining it used to make me cry with the sense of loss and grief.

### ❖ *I don't want to be solitary; I want to be in a fulfilling relationship*

Many of my women friends are divorced and single. The awful truth is that the odds are deeply against these women ever finding another love; most of the single men our age are chasing after women whom they could have fathered. A related concern is physical intimacy. I could not imagine having to find and retrain another partner! What Forrest Gump neglected to tell us is that sex is also like a box of chocolates. No matter what the man may look like all wrapped up and presentable, you never know what you're in for between the sheets! Especially in the "golden years"!

It came down to this: Divorce was not an option I could live with. And yet, we could not go on living together; years of misery had proved that. I needed a third option—an alternative solution to my distress.

## CHAPTER 10

# Setting Out

2007. So there I was, driving away from Cathie's office with her question echoing in my head:

*What are you modeling for your girls?*

I spent the next few days working that question. And then I did it. I started looking for another place to live. Although our finances had always been tight, I had come to realize that *one way or another, we had to live separately.* Either we could find a way to do it collaboratively and thereby save our marriage, or we would have to divorce. This travesty could not go on.

And it was clear that divorce would be a much more expensive option, both financially and emotionally. For all of us.

After doing some preliminary house hunting online, I worked with a wonderful realtor, a quiet, kind man, explaining that I was looking for a place for myself because I intended to separate from my husband. I explained that this all needed to be confidential, that he could only e-mail me or call my cell phone. I hated this sneaking around, but this was the way it had to be for now. I needed to wait for the right time to talk to Emil about this. And I needed to figure it all out. I needed to figure out what I wanted, what was realistic, what the best way to approach the subject with him would be.

The realtor and I looked at many properties and narrowed them down to a short list. The time had come.

# CHAPTER 11

❧

# Telling Him

E mil sat in his easy chair in the living room, reading one of his philosophy books. I approached him saying, "We need to talk." He put the book down and looked up at me.

I had given this moment a lot of thought. I knew that I needed to be calm and, even more importantly, kind. I didn't rehearse my lines; I didn't even know exactly what I would say. I just trusted that having worked this for as long as I had, the right words would come out.

I told him that I couldn't live like this anymore, nor did he deserve to live with the constant friction, bickering, and resentment that characterized our home life. I told him that I needed to get my life back. I explained that I had donated my life to the family, to the children, and now that they were grown, I felt that I had fulfilled the terms of my "contract." It was my turn.

I talked about my experience of our current situation. I talked about what I imagined he must be experiencing on the other end. *I did not accuse, I did not blame.* I acknowledged that we both had tried very hard to make it work and it was not working. I said that it had become clear to me that we were just not a good fit together: Apple and orange. Square peg, round hole. Country mouse, city mouse. And I pointed out that over the years, with all the bitterness and resentment and conflicting needs, we had gotten into very bad habits.

One of Emil's sterling qualities is that he is a very good listener when it counts. It's these moments when his heart comes out of hiding, when he opens up and is keenly present.

So he listened, without rushing to resist or defend.

"So what do you want?" he asked tentatively.

"I want to move out. I need my own place."

"Do you want a divorce?"

"No. I want to try to reinvent our relationship. I want to give us a chance to break bad habits. To have the space to sort out what's mine in this mess, what's yours, and what's left. As much as I can't stand you sometimes, I also know what a wonderful human being you really are. I remember why I married you. You're still that person, somewhere inside. I want us to have a chance to rediscover the people we once were."

He thought for a moment and offered, "Maybe we should try marriage counseling again."

"No," I replied. "Four years of counseling, every week, and we still keep doing the same old shitty things to each other. We keep repeating the same cycles. There's nothing new here. There are no new questions to bring to a counselor. It's time for us to just figure this out. And I can't stay in this house with you any longer."

He was quiet. His face looked pained, weary, as though he had been bested in a battle.

"So what do you suggest we do? You know I can't afford anything. I'm working as hard as I can. I don't know how long I can keep up this pace. I'm not getting any younger."

"Well," I replied, "I've thought a lot about it. I think we should buy a townhouse for me. I don't want to throw money away on a rental. And buying something would be a good investment for both of us. For almost ten years now you've been paying college tuition for the girls, and you've managed that out of your income, and now they're all graduated. So we know there is that much wiggle room in your cash budget. And I have been using my income for our vacations, gifts, fun, and nice things for myself. I am thinking that if we borrowed some money for a down payment, and you covered the mortgage, I could find a way to pay for the rest of my living expenses."

It made sense. Emil realized that getting a divorce would be much more expensive, and we had come to the point where that was the only alternative. He was willing to give this idea some consideration.

# CHAPTER 12

❦

# A Joint Venture

The next day, I introduced Emil to my realtor. We looked at a handful of places. Emil, ever the builder, inspected each one carefully and made an effort to humor me about the features that I valued most. Day by day we looked at more places, talked about the pros and cons. He was most concerned that we buy a place where I would feel safe.

Already I could see my prince coming out of exile.

And then he said, "You know, this is not going to work if you start seeing other men."

The idea of my beginning an intrigue with another man cut way too close to the bone for him, in view of his experience with his former wife. The notion of me even flirting with someone was enough to trigger all of his primitive instincts. Controlled rage was palpable just beneath the surface. He wondered whether I was using the line about "reinventing our relationship" as a ruse to get him to buy me my own little love nest. He started thinking about all the single men we knew. He warned me that they would be coming to court me.

And while I really didn't know what was to become of our

marriage in this uncharted territory, I did know that I was not interested in starting something new. And what I knew even more clearly was that I had not come across any other men in decades who were the least bit tempting to me.

So I could answer him clearly and with confidence, "I am not going to see other men. This is about us and trying to save our marriage. I am married to you and want to stay married to you. I want to find a way for us to have a healthy relationship, in spite of all of our differences."

So it was agreed. We would do it. We got the loan for the down payment and narrowed the list of places to a few favorites.

Then came the next threshold: how to tell the girls.

# CHAPTER 13

# All in the Family

We convinced Susanah to come home for the weekend without telling her why, which was exceedingly difficult. We felt it was important to tell her before telling the other girls, since she would be the most deeply impacted. We are her only parents; our home was her only home.

She was so brave. She sat there and listened. Though she appeared calm and collected, there was a deep, searching ache behind her eyes. She asked questions, we answered. Outward calm aside, I could tell that she was rocked to the core. It was as though her chronology had been suddenly notched. This was a demarcation. Her reality was shifting.

Susanah was twenty-one, recently graduated from college, and working as a research assistant for one of her professors. She had been pondering her future, deciding how to launch her life. This change in her family constellation would prove to be a deep severing of the ties to childhood.

Later that evening we called Lisi and Julie, who were both living nearby, and asked them to come for breakfast the next morning, telling them that Susanah was in town. We didn't reveal our true purpose.

We set the breakfast table out on the deck and, as we started to eat, Emil began the telling. Eating stopped; no one was very hungry anymore. Lisi and Julie listened, stunned. Then Julie jumped up and ran to the bathroom. I went after her. I found her huddled on the floor, weeping. I held her. Between her sobs, I heard her say, "You better never leave me!"

"I'm not leaving anyone," was my reply.

We went back to the table. We all cried. I talked about how this had come about and what my hopes were: we needed to re-invent our relationship. And I said to the girls, "I hope you won't be mad at me. I couldn't bear the thought of losing you," which brought a fresh flood of tears.

At last, as the tide of tears began to ebb, Lisi said, "You know, I am the opposite of disappointed in you two. This is a very brave thing you're doing." These words from her were all the more meaningful considering that she had just become engaged to the love of her life.

An hour later we were in the car driving the girls around to see the places we were considering. Julie found a four-leaf clover in front of one house. A few weeks later, we put down our first payment on that place.

# CHAPTER 14

# Our New Life: Some Things Lost, Some Things Gained

2010. Three years have gone by since that eventful summer. Emil and I have forged our new path in a very gentle and organic way. There have been no rules or regulations or fixed expectations, except truth and fidelity.

Emil gave me a tremendous gift in this new phase of our marriage: he let me set the tone. He knew that I needed to regain sovereignty over my life and has allowed me all the space and time that I need. This has not always been a predictable process. In fact, when we closed on the townhouse and moved my furniture in, I asked him if I could still stay at "his" house for another week or so. He said, "Sure." I wanted to have the time to make my new place into a home before I took the step of living alone for the first time in more than twenty years.

Since then, our arrangement has evolved into a fairly regular rhythm:

❖ We spend Friday and Saturday nights together and sometimes Thursday or Sunday—usually at his house, but sometimes at mine. I sometimes go out with friends on these evenings, but come home to his house afterward.

❖ He comes over to my place for dinner once or twice during the week, and I cook once or twice on the weekends. We go out for a soup-and-salad dinner-date once a week too, often combining it with grocery shopping.

❖ We talk on the phone nearly every day.

❖ He takes an active interest in maintaining and fixing up my place. After all, we co-own it; it's an investment.

❖ I help him with cleaning and gardening at his house.

❖ He pays the mortgage and the car insurance, and I pay the rest of my monthly expenses.

❖ When Susanah is in town, we try to all stay together in one house.

There are things we've had to give up for this arrangement, such as spontaneous cuddles and being there for each other if an emergency arises. Emil misses having a resident cook and housekeeper. I miss having spending money. I miss my perennial gardens and being in my family's home.

But we've also been able to give up other things: getting on each other's nerves and battling over living space, food choices, and how we spend our leisure time. There are still friction points, to be sure. Living separately did not magically make us perfectly compatible. But now the arguments are very few and far between and happen without the hair-trigger effect. And we always have the option to say, "Maybe I should just go home. We can try again tomorrow."

And there's one more thing that was lost: forty pounds. Being in my own space and reclaiming dominion over my life has given me the strength, independence, and impetus to remodel my body too.

What have we gained?

We have gained a renewed respect and appreciation of each other. Having our own spaces where we can nurture ourselves has enabled us to release all the bitterness. Perhaps most importantly, we have rediscovered compassion and generosity for each other. There is tenderness now.

We have relearned how to enjoy one another. We go for walks in the woods. We wander through the bookstore, leafing through books and magazines. We go to plays at the community theater. We stroll down the pedestrian mall, hand in hand.

We have been able to see more clearly what we are each creating in our own lives, both the problems and the joys. Now that we live apart, a bad mood isn't contagious. The toxicity is gone. Instead, we advocate for each other.

We have gained enlivened relationships with our children, who can now more easily see us as individuals trying to do our best in life. There is a new joy in our interactions with them. *They see us as strivers, not failures. They see our integrity, not our misery.*

And this is just the beginning. Life is full of opportunities and hope.

PART 2

The Family Speaks

*You've heard my version of the story. Perhaps you're wondering what the other members of our family think about all this. And rightly so! So I asked them each to write a passage about their experience of our family's evolution. As you might imagine, it was very poignant for me to read their accounts of our shared past. I have left them unaltered so that you may hear each one's true voice.*

# CHAPTER 15

❦

# Susanah's Story

Mommy and Daddy kept their problems largely to themselves. Well, the tone of their relationship wasn't exactly a secret, but they never involved us in their troubles by discussing their unhappiness or painting each other in a negative light. But it was clear to me pretty early on that my parents' relationship was not an example of "marital bliss." I caught myself wondering sometimes whether my parents could actually be in love—whether they ever had been—and how in the world they came to be together. But I just took it for what it was. It was what we had; it was our reality.

I remember the first time Mommy said anything (in my presence) about the beginning of their marriage and how she had considered taking me and moving away. And in spite of my own questions and doubts about their relationship, that first experience of hearing them confirmed was still unnerving. It's the sort of thing that makes you swallow really hard and wonder where things stand now. It makes you want to quell every argument and defuse every conflict in the act of self-preservation. I never let myself go so far as to think my parents would actually divorce, but I had quite a heightened sense that things could snap at any moment, that one day Mommy might decide she'd finally had enough. Mommy definitely seemed to be the variable in the relationship; Daddy seemed pretty unswerving.

I was uneasy when the counseling started—first with Mommy and Daddy together, and then the whole family. I remember sitting in the waiting room of the counselor's office while they had their session. The reason for their unhappiness was actually a mystery to me and I wondered what it was they were being counseled about. Were they really that upset? Was it really this serious? Should I be worried?

I had always had the sense that my parents were not much of a pair. They stood in especially stark contrast to my sisters' mom and her husband. It always hurt my feelings when Lisi and Julie would come home from vacation at their mom's house and, fed up with the bickering at our house, tell us about how much nicer it was at "Mommy's house" and ask, "Why can't we be more like them?" That stung even more than when my parents were mean to each other. Some of my most fragile moments were when I would go with Lisi and Julie to stay at their mom's house and would have to stand as the representative of my parents, of "our house," of that part of the blended family. I wanted to melt into tears during those moments when I had to defend my parents—us—against criticisms about their hardness. They weren't bad people for their unhappiness. It hurt me when they were esteemed unfairly.

And beyond that, they were my parents, my foundation, and though I didn't like the way they were with each other, I disliked even more the idea of them being apart. I didn't see our problems as stemming entirely from my parents' relationship; it seemed to be our whole family dynamic. We could all be pretty nasty to each other, so I felt like we all shared responsibility for the unhappiness in our house. My experience of our family therapy sessions was pretty nightmarish—everyone feeling like they had to defend themselves from each other.

In spite of all this, we did have many happy moments, and I generally look back on my childhood as pleasant and on our home as being warm and loving. For all the grumbling and hurt feelings, we laughed together a lot, we sang together, we admired each other for our individual gifts, and we hugged a lot.

I was really afraid of what my parents were going to tell me when I came home that June weekend in 2007. The whole two hours I drove from Williamsburg to Charlottesville, I went through all of the worst-case scenarios. I knew there was news waiting for me and I knew it wasn't good. Mommy was never that needy about wanting me to come home. It was clear that she was hiding something, and it made me really uneasy.

I was devastated when they told me they were going to live separately. "We're going to rearrange our family." I remember thinking, *We've already got the strangest family arrangement of anyone I know!* My heart sank into my stomach as the child in me thought, *God, now it's really happening.* I was scared mostly because I didn't know what it really meant. Even though they were talking about a new beginning, I was hearing an ending. It felt like something was breaking. I wasn't sure what we were losing, but I knew we were losing something. And the scary part was that none of us honestly knew how it would all pan out. At that moment, although my parents never seemed to fit together the way a couple in love should, their love for me felt very much tied to their love for and commitment to each other. Looking back, I guess I've always felt that way. Shaking up their relationship sounded like a threat to their relationship with me, too. I think I was afraid of losing that one great constant in my life.

Later that day, Mommy took me out to tour the houses she was looking at. It was of utmost importance to her that she move somewhere I would also feel comfortable living. It was clear that this would be a new home for me too. And though I was very upset that I was losing the integrity of my childhood home, and it was going to take me a while to reconcile myself to the fact that our old house without Mommy's presence in it was not going to be home, I got swept up in the excitement of this new adventure. I had always liked indulging in Mommy's dream plans—whether they were about converting the commercial wasteland near our house into a riverside café / art studio / community-gathering place, or building an addition onto the back of our house. Those images of transformation, of shaping our reality in the likeness of our dreams, fed my soul. It was that sense of newness and possibility that lent me confidence and hope in this "rearrangement."

Until recently, I think I largely regarded my family as little more than a backdrop for my life. In the last couple of years, it has taken on much more dimension. When I think about my family now, I see that if we are flowers, we are also each other's gardeners. We grow each other and have been grown by one another.

Family is our greatest opportunity to practice and experience unconditional love. Family is my most profound and indelible connection to human existence. Family is that from which I derive and to which I bestow. I am not me without my family. We are of each other and therefore always by each other. Family is my harbor.

It turns out that Mommy and Daddy's rearrangement was indeed an ending, but one that made way for a new beginning that has turned out to be much brighter than I think any of us could have imagined when taking those first tender steps. Whereas before, we were all more inclined to be a bit callous with each other, with this change in Mommy and Daddy's relationship, I have felt a tremendous shift within the whole family. Something has softened within us. Somehow we've been able to shrug off layers of defensiveness and self-preservation to become more tuned in to each other. We are more sensitive, more careful, more perceptive and receptive, more adoring of one another; we treasure each other for the precious family that we are. And we are tickled with wonder at who these *individuals* are that we've had within us all along. Something has been freed. And we are more robust.

I think what my parents are doing is the greatest gift they can give to our family. In doing something for themselves and for each other, they are doing something for all of us. The love and happiness they foster in their relationship permeates the rest of our family. Perhaps more than anything, they are modeling for us how we can and must shape our own lives in the best way we are able. They are demonstrating to us what is important—and at the same time, they are showing us that in determining what's important, convention should not be an impediment. They are creating the space and providing the impetus for us to grow, both as individuals and together, as a family.

Rather than walking away and scrapping what we had, we are building onto what we've already got. This is a tough lesson we have been handed, something very tempting to decline, but in choosing to stay and learn it, we are also reaping untold rewards.

CHAPTER 16

Lisi's Story

One of my favorite childhood memories of Daddy and Lise
is that once in a while, they would dance. Daddy liked to
make pancakes to Johann Strauss on Sunday mornings, and this
atmosphere caused his usual gruff, practical demeanor to give
way to a light whimsicality. Sometimes he would sweep Lise into a
goofy waltz within the five-foot square space afforded to them by
our tiny living room.

A few years ago I would have said that I cherish this memory
because it was so rare to even see them in such close proximity.
Now, with this re-envisioning of their relationship, it feels like
spring is here after a long winter. Imagine my surprise when, soon
after Lise's move, Julie gossiped excitedly to me on the phone, "He
even called her 'honey' the other day!"

This new spring is a far cry from the stinging air of the
Williamsburg hotel room that Lise, Daddy, and I shared during
Susanah's graduation festivities in 2007. I did not realize how
bad it was until that day. I had grown up with the accusations
and the sarcasm, but that weekend it got to a point where I was
embarrassed and even insulted that they would behave so bitterly

to each other in front of another person, even if it was their own daughter. Come to think of it, especially if it was their daughter. Therein lies the tragic thing about a "contract marriage" without romantic love. Though the parents may be staying together for the kids, the kids feel it—the negativity affects them profoundly, even when it has become a regular part of everyday life.

Lise's generation may have imagined the ideal marriage as a fairytale, but because of how I saw my parents experience marriage, it was not a concept in which I was even interested as a young adult. Both my mom and dad have been through more than one marriage. In at least half of these cases, they got married after having known their spouse-to-be for only a matter of months. I grew up thinking of marriage not as "holy matrimony," but as an unnecessary contract between adults that often didn't work and was hard to get out of. Not that I didn't think I would find my prince someday; I just didn't think we would get married. We would just simmer together forever in unbound bliss. And if we did get married, it would be in our eighties as an afterthought.

As it turns out, for my husband Jack and me, marriage was the next chapter in what has been a long relationship. Five years after having graduated high school together, we ran into each other at a concert and soon after began dating. We were in a relationship for five years before we decided to get married. Both of us saw the conception of marriage in our society as flawed. On the one hand, marriage was a sacred essential of life, but at the same time, many people seemed to treat marriage like a piece of clothing that could be discarded at will. It seemed hypocritical. Jack and I shared a deep awe of the almost unimaginable possibility of a true, respectful marriage. We discussed the possibility of getting married for a long time before we decided to go through with it or to even tell anyone we were considering marriage. One of the most important reasons for becoming legally married was our desire to eventually have children. We also wanted to make our devotion to each other clear to our families. If we were going to get married, we were going to be very serious about it.

The years that Jack and I spent together before we were married were invaluable to the quality of our first years of marriage. Another person is a whole world; there is so much to learn, and it takes time. I can't imagine how hard it must have been for Lise and Daddy, having known each other for only a short time, to be there for each other while trying to raise kids and make it financially. Jack and I have not had children yet and are fortunate to have time now to learn how to be individuals together while still sharing as much as we can. I hope that we still say "I love you" ten times a day when we have kids, and I hope they hear us.

Despite our complicated and at times unpleasant past, I am extremely proud of my family. Both sets of parents raised me to think and live outside of society's box. In high school, I got a subtle satisfaction from my friends' amazement when I told them that my parents were divorced but we all got together for Thanksgiving and Christmas. My parents have raised me with a strong sense of what is good and right to do. They have worked together instead of alienating each other, even when that would have been the easy road. Lise and Daddy's re-envisioning of their marriage is the furthest outside of the box we have gone, but I wouldn't expect any less from their true selves.

# CHAPTER 17

# Julie's Story

It was a lovely summer morning in Virginia. Our parents had called us sisters to the house for a Sunday brunch, and they were strangely secretive about their reason for celebration. I had assumed that we would be congratulating my sister on her recent graduation or enjoying a surprise for someone's birthday, but upon arriving and seeing the uneasy and strangely reserved expressions on my parents' faces, I knew they had something completely different in mind. As Lise began to explain their plans for buying a new house—but only for her—I burst into tears and ran into the bathroom, too emotionally jarred to actually hear what my stepmother and father were planning to do. *Here it is*, I thought, *Susanah has graduated and they are finally getting a divorce. Lise's gonna leave me. I hate change; I can't take another change to our family structure!* Little did I know that this change would usher in a new and positive existence not just for our parents, but also for our entire family.

Growing up with divorced parents was a very difficult and often painful experience for me. I loved both of my parents dearly and wanted to be with them both all of the time. I loved my father for his dependability and stability and his quiet adoration. I loved my mother for the happy, free, and loving environment she favored in her household. As time went on and I was forced to spend more time at my father's house, a great imbalance started to occur. I longed for my mother and her happy, hippie, fairy self and started to resent my father and stepmother for their hypercritical and overbearing way of life. This dichotomy occurred both because I was staying with my mother only on vacations, when life was fun and carefree, and also because of the unhappiness that was so present in Lise and Daddy's marriage.

As a child, of course, I tended to think of my parents not as unhappy, but rather as mean and strict. I felt like it was my fault they were mad all the time. I started to build up great defenses against the sarcasm and criticism and, in turn, became deeply critical of myself. My father and I butted heads a lot when we sisters were growing up, and I remember Lise acting as the mediator in many of these situations. I used to be afraid of having people over at my house for fear that our family dynamic would scare them. I was pretty sure that most families were a little happier than ours, and that most parents didn't speak to each other the way my stepmother and father did. I was sure of it, because my mother and stepfather didn't act that way.

Something that used to always stick out in my mind was that when Lise went away on a trip, Daddy got so much nicer and was less critical and whistled and sang around the house a lot more. I always wondered at the fact that I got along with my father better when he was alone, and I attributed it to the fact that he got to be all-the-way in charge. I didn't usually take trips with Lise without Daddy, but I remember a peace about her when she returned from these trips, and though I noticed this, being a dreamy child, I didn't think much of it. Until I was quite a bit older, I never really thought that Lise and Daddy would get a divorce or really had problems. I thought that the way they were was how they liked it.

I didn't think it would ever really change—or maybe I thought it would change when we all moved out.

Though I was initially shaken about the idea of my father and stepmother living in separate houses, I soon began to understand why their choice was a very positive one—why it made so much sense. Lise liked things neat and tidy, and Daddy tended to turn all available space into part of his workshop (I can no longer walk into my room because of the piles of toolboxes now coexisting with my stuffed animals). Also, as the process got underway and we all got used to the idea, Lise and Daddy seemed to argue less, and we all started to gain a newfound respect for one another as individuals in a spiritually growing family.

Last year, I had the privilege of staying with Lise in her new home. I had been going through a rough time, and Lise opened her doors to me wholeheartedly. This immediate embrace conveyed to me Lise's real commitment to the family. I also noticed, upon moving in, a kind of newfound vigor she now held to show each of us who she really was. I believe that having lived in a tough and unhappy situation in which her house was never really the way she wanted it and her ideals were not fulfilled, Lise lost a part of herself somewhere. She was unable to be the fun-loving woman of her past, and it only compounded her sadness that she couldn't show us how different she really was from the way we viewed her.

Since I moved in with my stepmother, I have had a complete perspective change. The Lise I grew up with, though caring and committed, was highly critical and often in bad or unhappy moods. The new Lise is quiet, kind, light, and oftentimes confiding. I have gone from having a stepmother whom I looked up to but was fearful of, to having someone whom I can trust not only to be there when I need her, but also to respect me as I respect her. I am happy to say that my stepmother is fun, funny, and beautiful.

And it doesn't end there. Lise and Daddy go on dates. They

hardly bicker with each other anymore, and it's nice to be around them! And Daddy seems much happier too. Though the duties of keeping two houses sometimes weigh on him, he is much lighter and more fun to be with. He has gotten into growing herbs, eating even more healthily, and filling his house with as many tools as he needs! He is much happier, and I'm pretty sure he has said "I love you" to me more times in this chapter of his life than in the whole previous twenty-eight years of mine!

# CHAPTER 18

# Emil's Story

W hen I think back and wonder why I married Lise, I realize that, behind the veil of the first infatuation, she was a lovely and very intelligent woman to me. Further, we shared the same spiritual outlook, which became more and more important to me as time went on. She also loved children and had an innate way of engaging them so that they wanted to be with her. And I had two children who definitely needed love and structure in their young lives.

After some time of being married, the differences between us began to be more and more apparent. Our temperaments were at opposing ends of the scale, it seemed, with me being the more easy-going, choleric type, and she the deep-feeling, long-nurturing, more slow-moving, heavier soul. Soon the undercurrent of our different backgrounds made itself felt: I had grown up on a farm in Europe, she in an American city, and there was that hint of American superficiality in her approach to many things.

In the early months of our marriage, Lise became devastated by the perceived distance and coldness emanating from me. For weeks and months she was more or less bathed in tears, whereas I tried to stay calm and collected, unruffled, which probably made things worse. I thought we could ride this thing out, having grown up in a family where there was never a question of splitting up. Lise complained that I did not spend enough time with the family and that I was too concerned with my work. It just never seemed quite enough for her. We also clearly brought out each other's childhood pains and deficiencies.

I appreciate now that Lise tried to make ours into more than just a minimally functional marriage. She asked that we go for counseling, and I went along for four years with a very apt psychotherapist who, for all intents and purposes, saved our marriage. That experience enabled us to keep things relatively harmonious throughout our children's school and college years.

When the last one had graduated from college, we were fully facing each other without the children as a common task. Lise came to me saying that she needed a place of her own.

It was reminiscent of losing my former wife. But that was only a reflex, for I realized pretty quickly that this was different. I realized that Lise was deeply honest and genuine, and that made it an above-board dealing. We could work things out rationally.

And yet I had misgivings. I was worried that certain other men might want to court her. I was concerned that people might think less of me.

So I did not really like the idea at first, but I realized that Lise was too unhappy with the situation at my house. She felt like she was living in the middle of a contractor yard. Besides, we had tried to patch things up before just to find that the patches did not hold. I thought that living in two houses might really work out.

So we started looking at places, comparing houses—which places needed the least work, which were safest and rather close to ours. It was a lot of fun; we had a project together (maybe we should just have gotten a dog...).

Then she moved out. Since we both became more frugal and Lise pays most of her bills while I pay the mortgage, it has worked out fine financially. In fact, my bank accounts are healthier than they've ever been, despite the tough economy.

Living by myself during the week has been mostly enjoyable since I am active, busy, and engaged. I have a lot of contact with people through my work. I am self-sufficient and have plenty of things I like to do, so I am not dependent on Lise for entertainment. She often goes out with her friends, but we are mostly together through the weekends.

The downside of living by myself is that now I have two houses to keep in good repair. Also, I rarely cook for myself, and my own house is not as clean as I would like it to be.

When I go to Lise's house, I feel as if I am entering the soft part of my soul. It is the part that would be given to the finer things of life: reading, relaxation, entertainment, discussion. What is missing is the milieu of the farmer: a big yard, a sizeable garden, a workshop full of tools, etc.

Our relationship has improved considerably. We rarely argue at all, we are affectionate, we choose our outings carefully so we both can enjoy them (nature walks, star-gazing, eating out, concerts). We are now much more supportive of each other and do things for each other. I make or fix things for her, while she cooks for me or helps me clean house or plant flowers.

An unexpected bonus of this new arrangement is that since she has been out from under my controlling influence, Lise has lost a great deal of weight (about which I am very happy!).

Looking back at this enterprise, I think it has made me stronger. I am not drained by constant dissonance. I also feel stronger spiritually; I have weathered another storm in my life. I am depending more on myself, and I feel that I have done the right thing. Yes, there are times when I miss her, especially after we have had a nice weekend together. But overall, I am more efficient in my daily pursuits.

I also believe that this change has strengthened our relationships with our children, who may have reason to be proud that we have saved our marriage.

I am glad that we had the courage to make this change. It feels right on many levels. These days, I am proud to talk to people about what we've done. I hope that it will inspire others to find creative ways to mend their marriages.

PART 3

Greater Considerations:
Updating Our Concepts of Marriage

❧

# CHAPTER 19

# Why is Marriage So Hard These Days?

"50% percent of first marriages, 67% of second and 74% of third marriages end in divorce," according to Jennifer Baker of the Forest Institute of Professional Psychology in Springfield, Missouri.

Why is it so hard to stay married these days? The answer is of course, very complex, but I will attempt to address several factors that occur to me:

### ❖ We are not taught effectively how to be well married

How do we learn to be married? For the most part, we learn from what has been modeled for us by our own parents, by our community of extended family and friends, and, more than we'd like to admit, by Hollywood. This instruction is not didactic; it is not composed of rules or maxims that we file away cognitively. It is absorbed into our subconscious, where it takes form in our desires, attitudes, and habits. I have discovered in my own life that, despite my conscious railing against the thoughtlessness or foolishness of my parents, their patterning was ingrained in me from a very young age. And many of us who have attained middle age will confess that we are alarmed at the ways in which we are becoming our parents.

What was modeled for me and for Emil?

My family of origin was a very dysfunctional one. My parents seemed to hate each other. I don't recall a single moment of tenderness between them. It was cold war, virtually all the time. It seemed that they rarely spoke to each other, and often used me as a go-between. They finally divorced when I was fourteen. When my mother told me of their plans, my response was, "It's about time."

Growing up in that environment did two things: it made me determined not to marry the wrong person, and it inflated my fantasy of the perfect marriage to fairytale proportions. If I was going to get married, it was going to be flawless. I knew better than to make the mistakes that my parents had made. As a result, I spent my youth very consciously assessing a long parade of would-be husbands, casting each one aside at the slightest sign of incompatibility.

Emil grew up on a farm in Germany, the son of countless generations of village folk who worked the fields and kept livestock to maintain their living. His parents had a pragmatic, working relationship. There was no outward affection, no real tenderness between them, but there was a rock-solid understanding of marriage as the foundation of the family, the community. They each played their roles, and quietly but deeply respected each other for it. It was a no-frills arrangement, but it got the job done. Thus, Emil's notions of marriage centered on sharing the same goals and figuring out who would do what to make the household work.

These two models of marriage were not uncommon in our parents' generation. But we baby boomers were bound to ask for more. We had grown up in a time of questioning traditions and of celebrating individuality and freedom of expression. The old forms of marriage were not going to bind us.

❖ *We are more individual, as individuals, than we used to be*

Everything in modern culture is geared toward cultivating the individual. We have more choices in almost every arena than ever before. We are encouraged to discover who it is we really are and to find fulfillment of our personal dreams. This trend is good and essential for the evolution of the human being, but it can be at cross-purposes with being in a relationship. We have become keenly aware of our own individual needs and desires, and even more aware of them when they're not being met.

Further, as a person matures and gets older, his or her personality is refined. Whereas when we are young, we are so much a part of the pack, as we get older, our individuality gradually comes to definition and continues to do so throughout our adult years, not unlike the maturing of a fine wine.

When we are young, it is easy to be in a relationship. When we are older, it is more challenging. I have an image of hedgehogs: as pups, they are soft and cuddly; as adults, they have sharp edges.

In the context of all of this individuating, it's a wonder that anyone in our modern society can sustain a marriage relationship. And it's been my observation (and experience) that we often sacrifice some of our individual growth in order to maintain some harmony in a marriage relationship.

As human beings, we are evolving. Our concepts of marriage must also evolve. I am certainly not advocating that every marriage end up with separate living quarters; that would be absurd. But new forms of marriage must have room for the individual to find expression and fulfillment, while retaining the bond of love and commitment. We must learn to regard and honor each other as growing individuals, not just as "the wife" or "the husband" with traditionally delineated roles to play and functions to perform in each other's lives.

### ❖ We have unrealistic expectations of marriage

We often find that once the honeymoon is over, our spouse is not fulfilling all of our expectations. Many of us become disappointed, even bitter, as a result. Many of us struggle desperately to change our spouses into the people we need them to be.

Ultimately, we are infinitely better off when we can find it in our hearts to leave our spouses in peace. We should let them be who they are, appreciate them for who they are, and find other ways to get our needs fulfilled—within reason and the rules of decorum.

For me, this has meant many things. For example: I go out dancing with my girlfriends, and some male friends too, while Emil stays home and reads. I often travel without him, going on trips with friends or one of our children. And I eat differently when I'm not with him; I can enjoy those decadent desserts more when I'm not under his watchful eye.

And in my own place, I can maintain a beautiful, clean, orderly environment, and invite friends and family members to come and enjoy it with me. Furthermore, Emil now has the right to have his home just as he likes it; I have nothing to say about it.

Through self-awareness and flexibility, and with the space that separate households provide, we can find ways to work on these superficial expectations of married life and arrive at a more harmonious, satisfying arrangement. But for me, there was a much deeper, more unconscious form of expectation at work as well: my need to feel loved wholly and unconditionally. This primal need surfaces through a recurring dream that I have. It comes with variations, but always has the same theme. It goes something like this:

*I am in a house in a dimly lit room. There are other people in other rooms, but I am alone in this one, with a man. He stands behind me. He is very, very tall and broad-shouldered. I can't see his face, but I know him, have always known him. He enfolds me from behind with his strong arms. He seems to whisper in my ear, but I don't hear words. There is fathomless love. He sees and knows me to my core, and he adores me. I feel totally embraced in his love.*

For years, this dream was my beacon, whispering to me that there was another love waiting for me out there. When I thought about my relationship with Emil and compared it to the feeling in the dream, I was bereft. At those times, I tormented myself, wondering how to get out of this miserable marriage, and more importantly, how to find my dream man. I wanted to be married to the perfect man and have the marriage that would make me feel complete and fulfilled.

I don't remember how it happened, but one day it dawned on me: My dream man was not a man at all. He was an expression of the divine, perhaps even my guardian angel. Others have suggested that he represents the divine masculine within me. What I was experiencing in my dream was not earthly love; it was divine love. And I realized that it was not only foolish, but also inappropriate to expect to find that kind of love in the human realm. Sure, you might feel it for a while—it's what makes courtship so intoxicating. When we are strongly attracted to another, perhaps we are seeing his or her divinity. But it rarely lasts.

As little girls, we weave our dreams of marriage with the silken threads of fairytales. However, what many people don't realize is that if you look beyond the surface, the true, old, archetypal fairytales are not really about a prince and a princess; they are about the human experience on earth, the quest for completion and union with the spirit.

*We will only find that depth of unconditional love when we realize our relationship with the divine. We need to let our spouses off the hook.*

### ❖ We aren't aware of the hidden agreements in the marriage

I'm not talking about the vows we exchanged on the altar. Those are only the tip of the iceberg. I'm talking about destiny. I believe that as human beings, we are spiritual beings having an earthly experience. Our lives were designed to help us learn deep, spiritual lessons. Nothing happens to us by accident; everything that happens has within it an opportunity to learn and grow.

At a certain point in the midst of my misery, I realized that I had made a pre-earthly contract with this family. And I realized that the main thrust of that contract was to raise our three children. I believe that the marriage relationship was, in fact, secondary in terms of my soul's purpose in this life.

Of course, this is only my story. Each person has made a different pre-earthly contract for life. But I think it's essential for each of us, at some point, to take stock of this and figure out what, in fact, his or her marriage is about.

What kind of marriage did you contract for? You can tell by looking at what you got, because on some level, you got what you asked for.

Did you opt for the "fairytale"? Some couples actually do get the fairytale marriage: love, affection, harmony. We think of these people as the "lucky" ones, and truly, it is wonderful to see and experience the harmony in their homes. But I suspect that these people have simply chosen to do their struggling in other areas of life, to learn soul lessons in other ways.

Or did you opt for the "mystery school"? That's the one where there's a lot of struggle in your relationship, but when you step back, those struggles teach you a lot about yourself and hopefully spur you on to becoming a better person.

Years after I left my parents' home, I looked back on their marriage with a more objective eye. And I was surprised to hear myself say that despite the fact that they outwardly hated each other, I thought they were fundamentally quite compatible. They were both smart and intellectually curious. They both had a good sense of humor and irony. They both liked to travel. They shared a love of culture and the arts.

When I thought more about this, I began to see that if they had been able to recognize and resolve their own issues, their marriage might have had a better chance. If each of them had been able to slough off bad habits and transform hardened attitudes to reveal the bright, shiny souls inside, they might have been happy together. If they had looked at life and their relationship as a mystery school, they might have done the work that would have enabled them to grow as individuals and as a couple.

Or did you choose the "service contract"? This is the one I seem to have chosen. Apparently, I chose to dedicate my married life to serving our children. In retrospect, I should not have been surprised. In the years just before I met Emil, I had discovered my spiritual path. Part of that discovery included setting ideals for my life. My ideal was to be a channel of blessings on the earth, to be of service. My daily prayer was to serve others. I got what I prayed for.

Of course there's nothing cut and dried about these "options." There are infinite variations, and they can be intertwined. But I think it's helpful to take some perspective on what it is we have determined to do with our lives and our marriages, on a spiritual level. It helps us be more realistic in our expectations.

CHAPTER 20

❧

# Forging a New Paradigm: Not Your Mother's Marriage; Not Your Mother's Divorce

When our parents got married, marriage was a narrowly defined institution sheathed in generations of tradition. It was something that everyone did when they grew up. And everyone did it in pretty much the same way, without much questioning.

But we don't want our parents' marriage anymore. What do we want in contemporary marriage? In contemplating this, we can think about the features of a good marriage and the container in which those features might come to fruition. Of course each relationship will be unique. But here are some features that I think all healthy marriages should contain:

❖ A willingness to regard and respect each other as individuals

❖ A desire to support each other's personal spiritual growth

❖ A fundamental fondness for each other and enjoyment of each other's company (good chemistry!)

❖ Shared values and ideals (this needn't mean having the same religion)

❖ Shared views about raising children

❖ Truthfulness and trust

❖ Fidelity—a commitment to the bond between two people

What about the container? What can a successful, creative marriage look like? The answer is as varied as the individuals who set off on the venture. And that's the point. The old forms are outdated. We need to take up the challenge of building our families with creativity and intentionality. This book has described the self-designed "container" that Emil and I have created for our marriage.

Despite my proposal for re-inventing the forms of marriage, I still believe in weddings and vows. There is something transcendent in these rituals that brings our commitment to each other into deeper, richer, more sacred territory. A wedding ritual invites not only the family and the wider community, but also the spiritual realm, to support and nurture the bond of marriage.

As human beings, it is essential that we value and explore our relationship to the transcendent. Living consciously within the context of our spirituality brings us into a dynamic union with the streams of destiny that will lead us into growth and health.

On the other side, there's the divorce piece. If the marriage isn't working, something needs to shift. In our parents' generation, when someone had enough of their dysfunctional marriage, divorce was the way out. They went to the lawyer, the relationship shut down, the legal settlement was drawn up, the court made determinations. The bond between husband and wife was irrevocably violated; the family dynamic was shipwrecked. The individuals involved—

husbands, wives, children—were left to stagger away from the ruin and try to get on with life as best they could.

Divorce has become so commonplace, but is it really the only alternative?

No, of course not. Here I am presenting you with another option. In our "disposable" society, let's not take our damaged relationships out with the trash. Let's make the effort to value what is still good and worthy in our marriages. We can find ways to redesign the containers of our marriages that will go a long way toward eliminating dysfunction and unhappiness.

When I contemplated leaving Emil, I always had to come around to asking myself, "Then what?" What would life offer me on the other side? I couldn't envision finding another man with whom I would have so much in common. In fact, if I were to place a personal ad listing the qualities that I valued, Emil would pretty much fit the bill. So what about learning to value what I already had? Waste not, want not, as they say.

Don't discard the marriage; redesign it. Collaboratively.

# PART 4

# Could Living Separately Work for You?

CHAPTER 21

❧

# Some Criteria to Consider

Are you in an unhappy marriage? Are you desperate to do something, but not sure what to do?

*Do you need a divorce, or is it rather that you need to get your life back?* If you're unsure of the answer, I suggest trying the following:

## ❖ *Write a mock personal ad*

Include everything you want in a mate. Then look at it and pretend you've never met your spouse (take a deep breath and try really hard!). If you were just meeting him/her for the first time, how much of your ad would he/she embody? It can be difficult to be objective enough to see this clearly, so you might want to ask a friend to help. If you find that your spouse embodies at least half of your criteria, it's a good sign that there's hope (the chances of meeting a stranger who fulfills that much or more are fairly slim).

## ❖ *Look at the balance sheet of your marriage*

▼ *Staying married but living separately may work if*

▶ You remember why you wanted to marry your spouse

and you can still see glimmerings of those qualities in him/her;

▶ In between the hard times you have moments of fun and warmth together;

▶ You have some shared ideals or religious/spiritual beliefs;

▶ You can find a way to talk reasonably with your spouse, without blaming and accusing;

▶ The integrity of your family is very important to you.

▼ *Staying married but living separately may not work if*

▶ Your spouse is abusive;

▶ Your spouse is unwilling or unable to approach things with an open mind;

▶ Your respective outlooks on life are completely incompatible;

▶ You or your spouse is already invested in a new relationship;

▶ Your foundation of trust in each other has been irrevocably violated.

If the balance tips in favor of forging ahead with restoration, get ready to get started!

If, however, it goes the other direction, I am sorry. I would be false if I were to try to claim that all marriages can be (or should be) saved. But what I can offer is this: There is always a high road. There is always the option to salvage a bad relationship, even if you can't keep the marriage intact. It may take years, or even a couple of lifetimes, but you can find your way into the right relationship with your spouse. The key is to strive to hold him or her in the highest light, to understand his or her pain, to see through the diminished persona of your challenging spouse to the spiritual core. Because deep within each of us is a loving person who truly wants to do the right thing. It's just that sometimes life is so hard that we shut down. Try to be tender with yourself and your spouse as you do what you need to do.

CHAPTER 22

Living Happily Ever After, Separately:
How to Get There

Assuming that you found at least some criteria upon which to
renew your marriage, and you believe that living separately
could be an answer for you, now you need to take stock and make
plans. Here are some suggestions:

❖ *Seek professional help*

If you're not already working with a therapist, seriously consider
doing so. Anytime we approach life changes, it's important to have
a support system in place. This book may give you inspiration, but
it won't be able to walk you through the process. Translating ideas
into action, shifting your reality, can be very painful. It's good to
have help. A good marriage counselor is a godsend. If your spouse
is not willing to go there, find a good individual counselor, one
who will listen, help you sort through your "stuff," and support
you through your process.

## ❖ *Take inventory*

Spend some time thinking deeply about your marriage: what's wrong, what's right, and what's left. Journaling helps, and talking with close friends does too. Make a written list:

▼ *What are the things about your spouse that you appreciate?*

Reliability? Integrity? Kindness? Generosity? Fun?

▼ *What are the things about your marriage that you value?*

Security? Comfort? Connectedness?

▼ *What are the aspects of your marriage that are not working?*

What needs to go out with the trash (or, better yet, be "repurposed")?

## ❖ *Imagine a happier you, a happier spouse, and a better relationship*

See if you can create an image of your spouse at his or her best, happiest, healthiest, without all of the bad habits that have developed over the course of your marriage. Imagine your spouse's shining soul. Do the same for yourself, imagining your most kind, loving, joyful, strong, fulfilled self. Now imagine a relationship between you without stress, without struggle. It may help to remember what you both were like in your courtship days. Hold these thoughts and write them down. These are the images that you will have to refer back to and steer toward as you work to reclaim your life and transform your marriage.

❖ *Look at your finances*

Accept that for most people, living separately will require some significant belt-tightening, but it's not impossible (bear in mind that divorced people HAVE to do it!).

▼ *Think about ways you can economize*

    ▶ Keep driving the old car or trade down for a less expensive one. Plan outings that accomplish a number of things in one trip to cut down on gas and time.

    ▶ If you need new clothes, shop at consignment stores or on eBay.

    ▶ Sell clothes you don't wear anymore to consignment stores or on eBay.

    ▶ Cut down on eating out. Make soups or casseroles in big batches and freeze leftovers to use for future meals.

    ▶ Buy food from farmers markets or the bulk section of your grocery store.

    ▶ Discover the joys of low-budget fun:
- Walks with friends
- Gardening
- Evenings at the bookstore/café
- Playing cards and board games
- Looking at old photo albums and reminiscing
- Making your own simple jewelry
- Sewing and knitting your own clothes and gifts
- Matinées or pay-what-you-can night at the theater

▶ Celebrate the romance of living with less. As we settle down and grow older, we often begin to accumulate luxuries like multiple cars, an abundance of clothes and household items, "toys," and so on—sometimes in an attempt to satisfy a deeper lack. Yet many of us are nostalgic for the carefree feel of our youth. Rather than viewing cutting back on certain luxuries as a sacrifice, try to look at it as an opportunity to unburden. As long as you're reimagining your life to achieve deeper happiness, look around and ask yourself if there are nonessential expenses in your life that are contributing to more stress and dissatisfaction than joy. An extra vehicle and its insurance? Cable TV that distracts you from more meaningful pursuits? A tendency to use shopping as therapy? An expensive collecting hobby resulting in "stuff" you don't really have a use for? Dare to imagine your life without these factors—it might just be better.

▼ *Figure out what sort of second home you can afford*

Emil and I were fortunate enough to be able to buy a townhouse; many people will instead be looking at rentals. That's okay!

▼ *Realize the cost of the alternative*

A lot of people will get stuck here and say, "We can't afford a second home." My reply: if you get a divorce, you will *have* to afford a second home. Living separately but married is a whole lot cheaper in the long run, starting with the fact that you're not paying for lawyers!

### ❖ *Begin the search for a new place to live*

Start looking around to get an idea of what's available, whether it's renting a room with a friend, renting an apartment, or buying a house. I did this alone before I talked with my husband about any of this. It helped me get a realistic perspective on what the possibilities were. It helped me feel hopeful that there truly was a way forward. And it enabled me to make an informed presentation to him when the time was right.

### ❖ *Tell your spouse*

▼ *Prepare*

Only you know what the right and best way to talk to your spouse is. You may not always hit the mark, especially when you're upset, but you know what works and what doesn't. Consider the following suggestions, but tailor them according to what you know of your spouse's moods, style, and likely responses. You might even get a friend to role-play it with you, having your friend represent you while you play your spouse. It can be helpful to do this so that you can anticipate his or her potential reactions and be prepared.

▸ Figure out the right time to tell your spouse. You've waited this long, so a few more weeks is not going to matter. Wait until after the birthday, holiday, or family vacation.

▸ Find a place of love and compassion within you. Remind yourself that your spouse doesn't like being in an unhappy marriage either. It's important to step outside of the anger and resentment, even if it's only for a while, if you're going to be able to talk with your spouse effectively. People who feel attacked or threatened shut down and cannot think creatively; it's a hard-wired biological response. A good way to open this conversation is to say something like, "You know, I realize that it must be really stressful for you to live with a wife/husband who doesn't seem to appreciate you…"

▸ Realize that unlike demanding a divorce, which you can do as coldly as you please, redesigning your marriage must be a collaborative undertaking. You must find ways to communicate openly and effectively with each other or it will not work.

▸ Once you've planned the timing, plan the setting:
  • Alone
  • Uninterrupted
  • Comfortable
  • A time when your spouse is relaxed and feeling content
  • Cup of tea? Glass of wine?

▼ *Topics that you may want to address are*

  ▸ Your experience of the marriage as it is;

  ▸ How it affects you;

  ▸ That you realize that this relationship must be hard for him/her too;

  ▸ That you want to get your life back on track in order to be healthy, happy, and effective;

  ▸ That you would be grateful for his/her understanding and help in this;

‣ The things that you appreciate about your spouse;

‣ The things that you value in the relationship;

‣ That you know he/she also deserves to be happy, appreciated, etc.;

‣ That you don't want to end the relationship, but redesign it;

‣ That in order to break old habits, heal, and have a chance to start fresh, you would like to consider living separately but collaboratively, at least for a while.

▼ *Give your spouse this book to read (with a marker at Emil's chapter!)*

### ❖ Give it some time

▼ *Let your proposal settle in for a while*

Allow your spouse to ponder what you've said for a couple of days. If he/she doesn't bring the subject up after that, find a good time to ask, "Have you given our conversation some thought?"

▼ *Tell your spouse more about what you've imagined*

Share your vision of what your lives and your relationship could be like. Talk about the strategies you've come up with for trying to make it work financially. If your spouse balks at the cost factor, remind him/her that redesigning your marriage would be far less expensive than divorce, in both financial and emotional terms.

▼ *Look at places together*

Talk about which one of you will live in the new place.

For Emil and me, it made sense for me to move out since our family home was also his business office and workshop space. Plus, it gave me the chance to finally get the fireplace I had been longing for!

## ❖ Consider the children

### ▼ *Grown children*

Our situation was ideal from the standpoint of the children, since they were all grown and out of the house. If this is the case with you, then you'll want to have a conversation with them as soon as you and your spouse have come to an agreement. Some things you might want to say include:

> ▸ That you don't want a divorce, you are not breaking up;

> ▸ That your desire is to redesign and enliven your marriage;

> ▸ That your relationships with them are sacred and should not be hampered by a new arrangement;

> ▸ That family time and traditions can still happen as before, but will be more harmonious and enjoyable.

### ▼ *Younger children*

If you still have children at home, the undertaking is much more complex. You will need to decide who will live where. You will need to provide guidance and a sense of constancy during the transition.

> ▸ I know of families in which the parents go back and forth from an apartment, while the children remain

in the family home.

▶ If you go the more common route, whereby one spouse lives with the children and the other one has his/her own place, it's important to have the new place include a warm, welcoming space for the children to visit and have overnights.

▶ Your explanation to the children should come after you've sorted out most of the details, so as to make it as clear and simple as possible.

▶ Don't fall into the trap of thinking that they should (or want to) help you make decisions. Now more than ever, they need the reassurance that their parents are a team and are taking care of them. The exception to this would be enlisting their help in designing their new bedroom in the second home.

▶ Help them to see that the family is staying together, but Mommy and Daddy need more space and some alone time.

▶ Be sure to plan lots of regular family time: dinners, outings, trips, even whole weekends just at home. This is a crucial way in which your situation is different from a divorce. The family is still intact, just living in two places.

# CHAPTER 23

# Into the Future

As you move forward with your new arrangement there are many things to consider:

## ❖ *Regarding space*

▼ *Do what you can to make the move into your new space exciting and joyful*

Help your spouse see the ways in which he/she will enjoy the space with you.

▼ *Be considerate when choosing which furniture and décor to take with you to the new place*

In our case, our family home had too much stuff, so it was a bit of a relief to divide it out. However, since I took the couch and easy chair, I made it a point to shop with him to replace them. I took the time to make sure that he was happy with the way his home looked when we were done. I found the other furniture I needed on Freecycle and Craigslist, two amazing online resources for low-cost (or free!) household items!

▼ *Work together to make the space work for you*

The spring after I moved, I realized that one way to ease my financial pinch would be to offer a home-based summer program for my nursery students. Emil saw that this would help me financially (which, in turn, would make him feel more at ease), so he installed a bathroom in the basement, as well as storage cabinets in the playroom. We got most of what we needed at the local Habitat for Humanity store. In our case, since we co-own both of our homes, any work that he does in my place is an investment in his future as well.

▼ *Offsetting the environmental footprint*

If you're someone who cares about the environment, you might want to think about what you can do to compensate for the extra space you'll be occupying. Emil and I have been "tree-huggers" for most of our adult lives, so the concept of each having our own home was a bit abhorrent. It helped to realize that for Emil, his house is also his home office, his workshop, and his industrial storage space, spaces that other builders would be renting out offsite. All things considered, though, we regard the environmental impact as a necessary evil and do our best to compensate in other ways. Emil and I are both rigorous reusers, recyclers, and Freecyclers. We also try to buy things in bulk, avoiding the waste of discarding empty containers. We frequently buy used things, especially furniture, clothes, and cars, and are very conscientious about turning off lights, keeping the thermostat down, and capturing gray water for laundry, plants, and flushing. I also have a listing on CouchSurfing.org, to share my guest room with travelers when I can.

## ❖ *Regarding time*

Deciding how much time you will spend together, and when, can be tricky.

▼ *Start out very simple and minimal*

‣ You can always add on more time together as time goes on.

‣ It's helpful at first to really get a feel for what it's like to live apart. This will be the most important step in helping you break bad habits in your relationship.

‣ Missing each other is a good thing. Giving voice to that feeling is even better. I have found that I even get a little excited when contemplating a night with Emil!

▼ *Structure your time together*

‣ Weekend overnights are a great way to begin rekindling the romance and enjoyment in your relationship.

‣ Talk on the phone regularly. Keep in touch and current with each other. Emil and I talk every day.

‣ Plan trips and getaways, even if it's just a day at the park. The more fun and joy you can bring into your time together, the more healing can occur.

## ❖ *Regarding needs*

▼ *Solitude*

It's important to be respectful of each other's need for alone time. Shifting your relationship will likely allow previously obscure (or forgotten) facets of your being to rise to the surface. It will be helpful to take the time to recognize, experience, and ponder them quietly. Give each other time to get to know yourselves again. If you find that you're in a bad mood for whatever reason, it might be a good idea to postpone that date together.

▼ *Togetherness*

One of the reasons that you're opting to live separately rather than divorce is because you value your connection to each other. This is an opportunity to put intention into that connection, to bring it out of the realm of habit and really appreciate it. Try to make your times together a celebration of that connection, rather than letting them lapse into the mundane. I have found that I am much more present with Emil when we're together now, since I don't take our togetherness for granted. Things like holding hands have much more meaning now.

▼ *Sex*

If your sexual connection has survived the troubles in your marriage, you're sure to find that living separately will only enhance it. Without getting into details, I will say that Emil and I have discovered a whole new lease on our sexuality! Being together can be like dating, but without having to wonder how far you can go. Some couples may worry that living separately may be frustrating. This is certainly possible, but as they say, absence makes the heart grow fonder! If, on the other hand, your marriage bed was not a happy one, this will be an opportunity to start over, taking your time to get to know each other again. It is crucial, in this case, that you have patience with each other and take things slowly.

❖ *Regarding friends and extended family*

▼ *Telling them*

    ▶ We told our close family members about our plans right away. They were a little incredulous, but supportive. As time went on and they saw that our extended family time and events were actually enhanced, not compromised, everyone was relieved. We even celebrated our daughter's wedding four months after I moved out. What a relief it was to be fully present and supportive of her and her new husband, rather than bitter and tormented by our dysfunctional marriage.

    ▶ We told our friends a little at a time, when we felt comfortable. We let the news permeate out gradually so that people would have time to figure out what was really going on.

▼ *Upholding the integrity of your choice*

It's important to be very respectful in the way you talk about your spouse and your arrangement with others. Whereas when you were in an unhappy marriage you might have done some grousing, rebuilding your relationship requires that you hold your spouse and your marriage in a warm and appreciative light.

▼ *Socializing*

    ▶ It's important that you are clear with others that

you are still married and not available. People will wonder whether living separately means that you now have an "open marriage." This may work for some, but it's my opinion that if you truly want to heal and fortify your marriage, you need to honor your fidelity to it.

▶ You will probably find that each of you will be spending more time with friends, which is good and healthy. I often go out with friends on a Friday night but go to Emil's house afterwards to spend the night. He's happy with this arrangement since he's not as gregarious as I am. There are also occasions when Emil has made plans with one of his friends at a time that I had hoped to be with him. I have to remind myself that he is entitled to do that and I have to accept it.

▶ It's important to be sensitive to and considerate of each other in this realm. It would be easy to lapse into game playing, such as trying to make your spouse jealous. Remember that your goal is to break bad habits and to foster growth and harmony in your marriage. Be open and truthful about your feelings with each other.

▼ *Sharing your experience and insights*

▶ You may find, as I have, that people are very curious about your undertaking. Talk to them about the gifts and the challenges in what you've done. But be careful to honor your spouse's sense of privacy. People often ask me how Emil feels about the arrangement, particularly since we separated at my behest. I make it a point to ask him the same question from time to time to ensure that I am accurately representing him to my friends.

▶ Join me in sharing your unique success story so others may benefit. Visit *www.lisestrykerstoessel.com* and let us know what worked for you!

# An Offering

*⟨══⟩*

I have given you a window into my life, my marriage, my family.
I have done so with a bit of trepidation over my loss of privacy,
but with a greater hope that my insights and experience might be
helpful to you.

I have not attempted to deal comprehensively with the subject
of marriage and divorce. Let the professionals do that. Nor have I
endeavored to give equal time to other perspectives. Let folks with
other experiences speak to theirs.

What Emil and I have done in living separately has healed so
much of what ailed us and our family. *It has not, however, made us
an ideal couple; that was not in the cards for us.* We still have warts and
moles. But our choice *has* enabled us to truly make the best of our
marriage. We are two people who are in some ways incompatible,
but we have found a way to preserve and strengthen our bond. We
honor each other in our differences. We don't try to reshape the
other in our own image anymore. We can live and let live. And we
love each other for the generosity of that gift.

Some friends have asked if we'll move back in together
someday. What might the future hold? My response: Who knows?
I can imagine that as we get older, it would be nice to have the
security of someone there in the next room, or beside you in bed
every night. Maybe we'll take that option. But in the meanwhile

we are doing what is right for now and leaving fears of the future aside. Life is indeed a mystery school. The key is to pay attention and work with what you have been given. Leave the future to itself.

What I have offered you is what I have been given: my experience, my stories, my hunches, and (hopefully!) my ability to relate these in a digestible manner.

Think of this book as a visitor. Imagine that someone has come into your home, and her presence has catalyzed new thoughts and feelings for you. She leaves without asking for anything, but her visit has stirred you. You are left in freedom. Freedom to ponder, to wonder, and perhaps, to act.

Thank you for letting me in. My wish for this book is that it may bring hope and healing to you.

May your path into the future be blessed.

# About the Author

Lise Stryker Stoessel earned her bachelor's degree in social welfare, specializing in mental health, from Stony Brook University in 1976. She received a master's degree in Waldorf Early Childhood Education from Sunbridge College in 2006. Lise has written articles and given numerous talks on a wide variety of issues related to parenting and self-development. *Living Happily Ever After—Separately* is her first book.